BASEL BÂLE BASILEA

Text: Rudolf Suter

Photos: Jean-Luc Iseli

Printed in Switzerland, 1984 by Imprimerie Bron SA, Lausanne

ISBN 2-606-00508-2

Basel

Die Geschichte der Stadt Basel lässt sich von prähistorischen Spuren an über keltische, römische, gallorömische Siedlungsreste bis ins frühe Mittelalter verfolgen. Eine erste urkundliche Erwähnung findet sie im Jahre 374 nach Christus. — Schon in karolingischer Zeit wichtiges Verwaltungszentrum unter einem Bischof mit namhafter weltlicher Macht, entwickelt sie sich zum bedeutenden Handelsplatz, vor allem dank ihrer günstigen Lage im Schnittpunkt alter europäischer Verkehrslinien. Zu eigentlicher Weltgeltung gelangt sie während des grossen Kirchenkonzils 1431-1448 und wird im Zusammenhang damit auch ein Zentrum des Humanismus und des künstlerischen Lebens (Universitätsgründung 1460, Erasmus von Rotterdam, Hans Holbein d.J.).

Mit der 1529 durchgeführten Reformation geht die politische Macht vollends an die Bürgerschaft über. Diese hat sich bereits 1501 für den Eintritt in die Eidgenossenschaft entschieden, deren spätere rechtliche Trennung vom deutschen Reich vor allem das Werk des Basler Bürgermeisters Johann Rudolf Wettstein ist (1648).

Im 17. und im 18. Jahrhundert lassen sich viele Glaubensflüchtlinge nieder und begründen u.a. die Seidenbandindustrie. In deren Gefolge blüht vor allem das Färbereigewerbe auf, und aus diesem entwickelt sich die chemische Industrie, die heute in einigen Sparten international führend ist. Ausserdem ist die Stadt Sitz zahlreicher Speditions-firmen, Versicherungsgesellschaften und Banken sowie ein Messe- und Kongresszentrum ersten Ranges.

Am deutlichsten spiegelt sich das Wesen Basels in seinem trotz allen Einbrüchen immer noch prächtigen Stadtbild, von dem die folgenden Seiten einen Begriff vermitteln wollen.

Rudolf Suter

Bâle

Des vestiges préhistoriques, des ruines d'établissements celtes, romains, gallo-romains évoquent l'histoire de Bâle jusqu'au haut Moyen Age. La première mention écrite de la ville remonte à l'an 374 après J.-C. Aux temps carolingiens, c'est déjà un centre administratif important sous l'autorité d'un évêque pourvu d'un grand pouvoir séculier. Bâle devient ensuite une place de commerce réputée. Elle le doit surtout aux avantages de sa situation de carrefour des anciennes voies de communication européennes. Le Grand Concile ecclésiastique de 1431 à 1448 lui donne une renommée mondiale. C'est alors qu'elle devient une capitale de l'humanisme et des arts (fondation de l'Université en 1460; vies d'Erasme, d'Holbein le Jeune).

L'adoption de la Réforme, en 1529, donne tout le pouvoir politique à la bourgeoisie. C'est elle qui, en 1501, milite en faveur de l'entrée de Bâle dans la Confédération, dont la séparation de droit de l'Empire germanique fut, avant tout, l'œuvre du bourgmestre bâlois Johann Rudolf Wettstein (1648).

Aux XVIIᵉ et XVIIIᵉ siècles, les réfugiés pour cause de religion affluent et introduisent la fabrication des rubans de soie. L'essor de l'industrie des colorants en fut la conséquence; il en sortit l'industrie chimique qui est, aujourd'hui, de classe internationale. De plus, la ville est le siège de nombreuses compagnies d'assurances, et de banques. C'est aussi un centre de foires commerciales renommées, et une ville de congrès.

Malgré toutes les atteintes subies, le magnifique visage urbain de Bâle est empreint de grandeur et c'est elle qui va paraître dans les pages suivantes.

Rudolf Suter

Basle

The history of the city of Basle can be traced from prehistoric remains through vestiges of Celtic, Roman and Gallo-Roman settlements right up to the early Middle Ages. It was first mentioned in records in 374 AD. As early as Carolingian times, it was an important administrative centre under a Bishop with considerable secular power and developed into an important trading centre, mainly as the result of its favourable site at the intersection of longestablished European trading routes. It took on worldwide importance during the great Ecumenical Council held there from 1431 to 1448 and, as a direct consequence of the Council, became a centre of humanism and artistic life (founding of the University in 1460, Erasmus of Rotterdam, Hans Holbein the Younger).

Following the Reformation in 1529, all political power passed into the hands of the burghers who had decided as early as 1501 to join the Swiss Confederation. This body's subsequent legal separation from the German Empire (1648) was mainly the work of Johann Rudolf Wettstein, mayor of Basle.

During the 17th and 18th centuries, many religious refugees settled in Basle and founded the silk-ribbon industry, among others. This was followed, in particular, by the dyeing trade which in its turn led to the development of the chemical industry which is now an international leader in some branches. In addition, Basle is the home of numerous carrier firms, insurance companies and banks, as well as of a world famous Industries Fair and a Congress Centre.

The essence of Basle is most clearly mirrored in its magnificent cityscape which has survived all inroads, and the next few pages are intended to convey something of its charm.

Rudolf Suter

Basilea

Le prime tracce della città di Basilea risalgono alla preistoria per continuare poi attraverso i secoli, ininterrotte e sempre più marcate, nei resti degli insediamenti celtici, romani, galloromani e del primo Medioevo. Il primo documento che parla della città risale al 374 dopo Cristo. Importante centro amministrativo già in epoca carolingia, governata da un vescovo esercitante un esteso potere temporale, la città si trasforma in un importante centro commerciale grazie soprattutto alla sua favorevole posizione, all'incrocio delle antiche vie di trasporto che attraversavano l'Europa. Sede dell'omonimo Concilio (1431-1448) Basilea diventa famosa in tutto il mondo allora conosciuto. Contemporaneamente essa assurge a luogo d'incontro privilegiato degli umanisti e degli artisti di tutta Europa (fondazione dell'università 1460, Erasmo da Rotterdam, Hans Holbein il Giovane).

Nel 1529, in seguito alla Riforma, il potere politico passa definitivamente nelle mani della borghesia, che già nel 1501 aveva dato un saggio della sua importanza, decidendo l'entrata nella Confederazione Elvetica. La separazione legale definitiva dal Regno di Germania, che avvenne più tardi, fu soprattutto l'opera del Sindaco della città Johann Rudolf Wettstein (1648).

Durante il XVII e il XVIII secolo Basilea accoglie molti perseguitati religiosi che danno vita all'industria della seta. Ad essa segue quella della tintura dalla quale, poco a poco, nascerà l'industria chimica, oggi internazionalmente all'avanguardia in diversi settori. La città è inoltre sede di numerose case di spedizione, società di assicurazione, di banche ed è anche un centro fieristico e congressuale di rinomanza mondiale.

La magnifica architettura, nonostante tutte le offese subite, ci permette di afferrare lo spirito di questa città che cercheremo di far rivivere nelle pagine seguenti.

Rudolf Suter

Rathaus. Mittelteil Anfang des 16. Jahrhunderts. Turm von 1900.

L'Hôtel de Ville (Rathaus) du début du XVIᵉ siècle. Tour de 1900.

Town Hall. Central section dating from the beginning of the 16th century. Tower from 1900.

Municipio. Parte centrale risalente al XVI secolo. Torre del 1900.

In majestätischem Bogen wendet sich der Rheinstrom zwischen den Stadthälften Kleinbasel (links) und Grossbasel von Osten nach Norden.

Les courbes majestueuses du Rhin coulant d'est au nord séparent le quartier du Petit-Bâle (à gauche) de celui du Grand-Bâle.

The waters of the Rhine curve majestically between the two halves of the city — Kleinbasel (Lesser Basle) on the left and Grossbasel (Greater Basle) — from the east to the north.

Disegnando un arco maestoso il Reno cambia direzione, da est verso nord, tra le due parti della città: Kleinbasel (a sinistra) e Grossbasel.

◁ Stets herrscht auf dem Rhein ein reger Schiffsverkehr.

La navigation sur le Rhin est toujours très active.

The Rhine always has plenty of shipping traffic.

Sul Reno regna sempre un'intenso traffico di battelli.

△ Die sonnige «Kleinbasler Riviera» lockt jung und alt zum Verweilen.

La «Riviera du Petit-Bâle», ensoleillée, invite jeunes et vieux à la flânerie.

The sunny "Kleinbasler Riviera" is a favourite spot with people of all ages.

La soleggiata «Kleinbasel Riviera» invita alla distensione giovani ed anziani.

◁ Im Rheinhafen anlegendes Güter-
transportschiff.

Navire marchand abordant au port de
Bâle.

A freighter docking in the Rhine
Port.

Una chiatta per il trasporto di merci
durante le manovre di attracco.

△ Personenschiff an der «Schifflände»
bei der Mittleren Brücke.

Navire pour voyageurs à la «Schifflände» (embarcadère) près du Mitt-
lere Brücke (pont du Milieu).

Passenger ship at the "Schifflände"
near the Middle Bridge.

Battello passeggeri alla «Schifflände», presso il ponte centrale.

◁ Zauberhafte Abendstimmung am Rhein.

△ Rhein und Kleinhüninger Hafenbecken I aus der Vogelschau.

Enchantement du soir sur le Rhin.

Vue à vol d'oiseau sur le Rhin et le dock I du Petit-Huningue.

Magical evening mood by the Rhine.

A bird's eye view of the Rhine and Dock I in Kleinhüningen.

Un incantevole tramonto sul Reno.

Vista aerea del Reno e del bacino portuale I «Kleinhüningen».

◁ Reger Güterumschlag an der Dreiländerecke.

Actif transbordement de marchandi-
ses au Dreiländerecke. (Jonction des
trois pays.)

Brisk goods transshipment at the
point where three countries meet.

Intenso scambio di merci al punto
d'incontro dei tre paesi : il «Dreiländerecke».

△ Blick vom Oberen Rheinweg auf eine
der schönsten Rheinuferpartien.

Vue du sentier supérieur du Rhin sur
une des plus belles parties des rives.

View of one of the most beautiful
sections of Rhine bank from the
"Oberer Rheinweg".

Una delle più belle rive del Reno
viste dall'«Oberer Rheinweg».

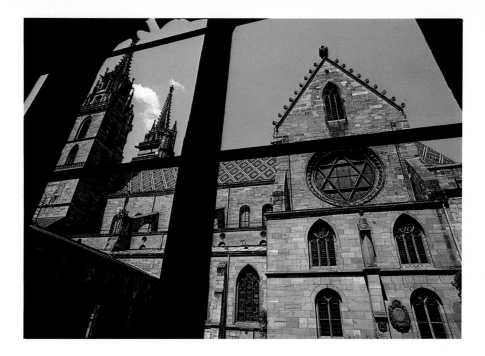

◁ Fasnächtlicher Tambour vor der Westfassade des Münsters.

Tambour du carnaval devant la façade occidentale de la cathédrale.

Carnival drummer in front of the west facade of the Cathedral.

Tamburo di carnevale di fronte alla facciata ovest della cattedrale.

△ Blick aus dem Kreuzgang auf Lang- und Querschiff des Münsters.

Vus du cloître, la nef et le transept de la cathédrale.

View of the nave and transept of the Cathedral from the cloisters.

La navata e il transetto della cattedrale visti dal chiostro.

◁ Sicht vom Münster auf Leonhardskirche (vorn), Marien- und Pauluskirche.

Vue de la cathédrale sur l'église
Saint-Léonard (devant) l'église Sain-
te-Marie et Saint-Paul.

View of the "Leonhardskirche" (in
foreground), "Marienkirche" and
"Pauluskirche" from the Cathedral.

Le chiese «Leonhardskirche» (davanti), «Marienkirche» e «Pauluskirche» viste dalla cattedrale.

△ Georgsturm des Münsters und Nord-
teil der Stadt.

La Tour Saint-Georges de la cathédrale et partie septentrionale de la
ville.

The George Tower of the Cathedral
and the northern sector of the city.

La torre campanaria «Georgsturm»
della cattedrale e la parte nord della
città.

Wettstein-Brunnen von A. Zschokke (1956) und Theodorskirche in Kleinbasel.

Wettstein Fountain by A. Zschokke (1956) and the "Theodorskirche" in Kleinbasel.

Fontaine Wettstein, par A. Zschokke (1956) et église Saint-Théodore, au Petit-Bâle.

La Wettstein-Brunnen di A. Zschokke (1956) e la chiesa «Theodorskirche» a Kleinbasel.

Detail der Westfassade des Münsters mit der Darstellung St. Georg mit dem Drachen (14. Jahrhundert, Kopie).

Détail de la façade occidentale de la cathédrale: saint Georges et le dragon (copie de l'original du XIVe siècle).

A detail from the west facade of the Cathedral showing St George and the dragon (14th century, copy).

Particolare della facciata ovest con la rappresentazione di San Giorgio con il drago (XIV secolo, copia).

Brunnenfigur (um 1400, Ko
auf dem Andreasplatz, bekle
ter Affe.

Le « Singe habillé », personn
d'une fontaine (vers 1400, coj
sur l'Andreasplatz.

Figure on fountain (around 1
copy) on the Andreasplatz,
thed monkey.

La scimmia vestita (1400
copia) della fontana sull'Andr
platz.

Braunbär im durch seine Zuchter-
folge berühmten Zoologischen Garten.

Brown bear in Basle Zoo which is
famous for its successful breeding.

Ours brun du Jardin zoologique
célèbre pour ses succès d'élevage.

Un orso bruno del famoso zoo cittadino.

◁ Wasserspiel von Jean Tinguely (1977) beim Stadttheater.

Jeu d'eau de Jean Tinguely (1977) près du Théâtre municipal (Stadttheater).

Jean Tinguely's original fountain (1977) near the Municipal Theatre.

Giochi d'acqua di Jean Tinguely (1977), presso il Teatro Municipale.

△ Oblicht-Pyramide des Stadttheaters und Turm der Elisabethenkirche.

Imposte-pyramide du Théâtre municipal et tour de l'église Sainte-Elisabeth.

Overhead light pyramid of the Municipal Theatre and tower of the "Elisabethenkirche".

Il lucernario a piramide del Teatro Municipale e il campanile della chiesa «Elisabethenkirche».

◁ Brunnen von 1547 vor dem Staatsarchiv von 1903 und Martinskirche.

Fontaine de 1547 devant les Archives d'Etat de 1903 et l'église Saint-Martin.

Fountain dating from 1547 in front of the City Archives (1903) and the Church of St Martin.

Fontana del 1547 davanti all'Archivio statale del 1903 e la chiesa «Martinskirche».

△ Brunnen von 1861 an der Verzweigung Gemsberg/Unterer Heuberg.

Fontaine de 1861 à la croisée du Gemsberg-Heuberg inférieur.

Fountain dating from 1861 at the "Gemsberg/Unterer Heuberg" junction.

Fontana del 1861, alla biforcazione Gemsberg/Unterer Heuberg.

◁ Der Nadelberg, einer der besterhaltenen Altstadtstrassenzüge.

Le Nadelberg, un des ensembles de rues de la ville ancienne les mieux conservés.

The "Nadelberg" one of the best-preserved series of streets in the old city.

Il «Nadelberg», uno degli angoli della città vecchia meglio conservati.

△ Ausstellungsbetrieb in den Hallen der Mustermesse.

Expositions organisées dans les halles de la Foire d'échantillons.

Exhibition bustle in the halls of the Swiss Industries Fair.

Intensa attività nei padiglioni della Fiera Campionaria.

Geborgenheit im Hof
Schmiedenzunft and der Ge[r]
gasse.

Intimité de la cour de la Cor[p]
tion des forgerons (Schmie[den]
zunft) à la Gerbergasse.

Sheltered tranquillity in
courtyard of the Smiths' Guil[d]
"Gerbergasse".

Intimità nella corte della cor[pora]
zione dei fabbri alla Gerberg[asse].

Das palaisartige «Blaue Haus» von 1768 am Rheinsprung.

La «Blaue Haus» (maison bleue) telle un palais, de 1768, au Rheinsprung (saut du Rhin).

The palace-like "Blue House" by the "Rheinsprung", dating from 1768.

Simile ad un palazzo, la «Blaue Haus» (1768), presso il Salto del Reno.

◁ St. Alban-Tor, Teil der mittelalterlichen Stadtbefestigung.

St Alban Tor, partie des fortifications médiévales de la ville.

St Alban's Gate, part of the medieval city fortifications.

La porta «St. Alban-Tor», parte delle fortificazioni medioevali.

△ Mittelalterliche Handwerkerhäuser am Rheinsprung.

Maisons d'artisans du Moyen Age au Rheinsprung (saut du Rhin).

Medieval craftsmen's houses by the "Rheinsprung".

Case di artigiani sul Salto del Reno, risalenti al Medioevo.

Blick vom Gemsberg zum Spalenberg.

Vue du Gemsberg sur le Spalenberg.

View from the "Gemsberg" to the
"Spalenberg".

Panorama del Gemsberg fino allo
Spalenberg.

Schulhaus am Kohlenberg, eines der relativ wenigen Basler Jugendstilgebäude. Davor Bronzeskulptur St. Georg von Carl Burckhardt.

Ecole du Kohlenberg. L'un des rares édifices bâlois de «Jugendstil». Devant, un saint Georges, bronze de Carl Burckhardt.

School building on the "Kohlenberg", one of the fairly few examples of "art nouveau" architecture in Basle. In front of it stands a bronze sculpture of St George by Carl Burckhardt.

La scuola sul Kohlenberg, uno dei non molto numerosi edifici Jugendstil della città. Di fronte, la scultura in bronzo di Carl Burckhardt, rappresentante San Giorgio.

◁ Das mittelalterliche St. Johanns-Tor kurz vor der Restaurierung 1983/84.

La St. Johann Tor médiévale, peu avant sa restauration en 1983/84.

The medieval St John's Gate just before its restoration in 1983/84.

La porta medioevale «St. Johanns-Tor», poco prima della restaurazione 1983/84.

△ Elefantenritt im Zoologischen Garten.

A dos d'éléphant dans le Jardin zoologique.

Elephant ride at the Zoo.

Una cavalcata a dorso d'elefante nel giardino zoologico.

◁ Fachwerkhaus am Rheinsprung, darüber Chor der Martinskirche.

Maison à colombage au Rheinsprung. Le chœur de l'église Saint-Martin.

Half-timbered house by the "Rheinsprung"; above it, the chancel of the Church of St Martin.

La «Fachwerkhaus», la casa delle arti e mestieri presso il Salto del Reno e, sovrastante, il coro della chiesa «Martinskirche».

△ Der idyllische Andreasplatz im Zentrum der Grossbasler Altstadt.

L'idyllique Andreasplatz au cœur de la ville ancienne du Grand-Bâle.

The idyllic "Andreasplatz" in the centre of the old part of Grossbasel.

L'idilliaca piazza «Andreasplatz» nel cuore della città vecchia di Grossbasel.

△ Hof des Bürgerlichen Waisenhauses, eines früheren Kartäuserklosters.

Cour de l'Orphelinat des bourgeois, anciennement couvent de chartreux.

Courtyard of the City Orphanage which used to be a Carthusian monastery.

Il cortile dell'orfanatrofio, anticamente un convento dei certosini.

Das Spalentor (14. Jahrhundert), ▷ bedeutendster mittelalterlicher Wehrbau.

La Spalentor (XIVᵉ siècle) la fortification médiévale la plus remarquable.

The Spalentor (14th century), the most important medieval defensive construction.

La porta «Spalentor» (XIV secolo), importante costruzione militare del Medioevo.

Flohmarkt beim Münster.

Flea market beside the Cathedral.

Marché aux puces près de la cathédrale.

Il mercato delle pulci presso la cattedrale.

ssburgerdenkmal (1895) und
-Hochhaus (1977) am Central-
nplatz.

Monument de Strasbourg
5) et la maison-tour BIZ
7) sur la Centralbahnplatz.

sbourg Monument (1895) and
high-rise building (1977) on
ntralbahnplatz".

monumento «Strassburger-
kmal» (1895) e il grattacielo
(1977) sulla Centralbahn-
z.

△ Restaurant «Zum Braunen Mutz» am Barfüsserplatz mit Malereien (um 1900).

Restaurant «Zum Braunen Mutz» (A l'Ours-Brun) sur la Barfüsserplatz. (Décorations 1900.)

The Restaurant "Zum Braunen Mutz" on the "Barfüsserplatz" with its paintings (round 1900).

Il ristorante «Zum Braunen Mutz» sulla Barfüsserplatz con le sue pitture (1900 ca.).

Die neuromanische Pauluskirche ▷ von 1901.

L'église néoromane Saint-Paul de 1901.

The neo-Romanesque "Pauluskirche" (1901).

La chiesa «Pauluskirche» del 1901, in stile neoromanico.

Das romanisch-gotische Münster, das alte Wahrzeichen der Stadt, aus der Vogelschau.

La cathédrale romane et gothique, antique emblème de la ville, vue à vol d'oiseau.

A bird's eye view of the Romanesque and Gothic Cathedral, the old city landmark.

Vista aerea della cattedrale romanico-gotica, l'antico simbolo della città.

◁ Der Badische Bahnhof von 1913, Bahnhof der Deutschen Bundebahn in Kleinbasel.

La gare badoise, de 1913, terminus des chemins de fer allemands au Petit-Bâle.

The "Badischer Bahnhof" (1913), the station of the German Federal Railway in Kleinbasel.

La stazione «Badischer Bahnhof» del 1913, la stazione delle ferrovie della RFT a Kleinbasel.

△ Bahnhofgebäude SBB von 1909 mit Centralbahnplatz.

Edifices de la gare des CFF, de 1909, sur la Centralbahnplatz.

The Swiss Federal Railway building (1909) with the "Centralbahnplatz".

La stazione FFS del 1909 con la «Centralbahnplatz».

◁ Die neugotische Matthäuskirche von 1896 in Kleinbasel.

△ Strassenmusikant in der Innenstadt.

L'église Saint-Matthieu néogothique de 1896 dans le Petit-Bâle.

Musicien ambulant dans le centre ville (Innenstadt).

The neo-Gothic "Matthäuskirche" (1896) in Kleinbasel.

Street musician in the city centre.

La chiesa «Matthäuskirche» del 1896 a Kleinbasel.

Musica nelle strade del centro cittadino.

◁ Vor den Arkaden des 1936 vollende-
ten Kunstmuseums.

Devant les arcades du Kunstmuseum
(Musée des beaux-arts), achevé en
1936.

In front of the arcades of the Art Gallery which was completed in 1936.

Davanti alle arcate del Museo di Sto-
ria dell'Arte (Kunstmuseum), termi-
nato nel 1936.

△ Eisenplastik von Chillida im Hof des
Kunstmuseums. Hinten Werk von A.
Calder.

Motif décoratif en métal, par Chil-
lida, dans la cour du Kunstmuseum.
A l'arrière-plan, une œuvre de A.
Calder.

Iron sculpture by Chillida in the
courtyard of the Art Gallery. In the
background, a work by A. Calder.

Plastica in ferro di Chillida nella
corte del Kunstmuseum. Alle spalle
un'opera di A. Calder.

Fasnächtlicher Trommler im Imbergässlein, an dem einst die Gewürzkrämer wohnten.

Carnival drummer in the Imbergässlein where the spice merchants used to live.

Tambour du carnaval dans la Imbergässlein où vivaient autrefois les marchands d'épices.

Tamburi di carnevale nella Imbergässlein, dove un tempo abitavano i mercanti di spezie.

Das Grossbasler Rheinufer mit dem mittelalterlichen «Seidenhof». Im Vordergrund die Fähre, die Passagiere von einem Ufer zum andern übersetzt.

Le «Seidenhof» (cour de la soie) médiéval sur la rive du Grand-Bâle. Au premier plan, le bac qui passe les gens allant d'une rive à l'autre.

The Grossbasel river bank with the medieval "Seidenhof" (Silk yard). In the foreground is the ferry which conveys passengers from one bank to the other.

La riva del Reno di Grossbasel con il «Seidenhof» (la corte della seta) risalente al Medioevo. In primo piano i traghetti che fanno la spola tra una riva e l'altra.

◁ Täglicher Viktualienmarkts auf dem Marktplatz.

Marché quotidien aux victuailles sur la Marktplatz.

Daily food market on the Market Square.

La «Marktplatz» con il quotidiano mercato di generi alimentari.

△ Rundhof eines der Mustermesse-Gebäude von 1954.

Rotonde de l'un des bâtiments de la Foire d'échantillons (1954).

Circular courtyard of one of the Swiss Industries Fair buildings (1954).

La corte circolare (1954) di uno degli edifici della Fiera Campionaria.

◁ Keramikmarkt beim Petersplatz während der Herbstmesse.

Marché de la céramique, lors de la foire d'automne à la Petersplatz.

Ceramic market on the "Petersplatz" during the Autumn Fair.

Il mercato della ceramica sulla Petersplatz durante la Fiera d'autunno.

△ Teil des ausgedehnten Messekomplexes: Rundhofbau von 1954.

Une partie du vaste ensemble de la foire: rotonde de 1954.

Part of the extensive Industries Fair complex: circular building dating from 1954.

Una parte dell'esteso complesso fieristico: Cortile circolare del 1954.

An den schon im Mittelalter grossen Brunnenreichtum erinnert u.a. der Spalenbrunnen aus dem 16. Jahrhundert mit seinen tanzenden Paaren.

La Spalenbrunnen, du XVIᵉ siècle, et ses couples dansant, évoque l'abondance médiévale des fontaines.

The 16th century "Spalenbrunnen" with its dancing couples is one of several examples of the numerous fountains which existed in Basle as early as the Middle Ages.

La Spalenbrunnen (XVI secolo) con le sue coppie danzanti ci ricorda la dovizia di fontane durante il Medioevo.

Printed in Switzerland, 1984 by Imprimerie Bron SA, Lausanne

ISBN 2-606-00508-2